LOVE & ALL ABOUT IT

Feel Love....... Like Never Before

RAHUL V. BHOLE

ISBN 978-93-5458-226-4
© RAHUL V. BHOLE 2021
Published in India 2021 by Pencil

A brand of
One Point Six Technologies Pvt. Ltd.
123, Building J2, Shram Seva Premises,
Wadala Truck Terminal, Wadala (E)
Mumbai 400037, Maharashtra, INDIA
E connect@thepencilapp.com
W www.thepencilapp.com

Author biography

A student at the <u>NATIONAL INSTITUTE OF FASHION TECHNOLOGY,</u>Rahul started writing from his teenage as a hobby which shaped itself into an everlasting passion.

He grew a fondness for Romanticism and Love which reflects in his work beautifully. Apart from writing, he is an avid Photographer with interests in fashion and wildlife and a musician by passion.

After his Debut book "Yaadein"which is a collection of Poems, he is all set to present you with another surprise of love.
Romance as a genre is something that has intrigued him and, his imagination helps him create a world as he likes.

He has co-authored 6 Anthologies with different publishing houses.

Follow him on Instagram-

Writing account - @inked_heights_

CONTENTS

Epigraph

"Writing is not just a hobby, it's a way to ink my thoughts into reality, and build an imaginary world "

- RAHUL V. BHOLE

Foreword

I have known Rahul for the past 9 years, that was even before he started writing. His passion for writing came to light after a couple of years when I saw a diary in his bag which was surprisingly full of poems and stories.

Since 2013, I have seen him experiment with most of the genres and write with different styles pertaining to his audience.
His interest shifted to romance as he went on reading books by various Indian authors. It took him some time to adopt a unique writing style that not only reflects in his Stories but is very well portrayed in his poem too.

His writing style is so creative that it gives you an image in your head as you read it. If Romance and love are something that interests you, his writings will surely connect to you in one way or the other.

Poems are always the best means to communicate your feelings in a sweet way while using fewer words to say more.
I have read a few of his works and they make you smile, they make you cry, they make you feel every emotion in a perfect manner.
His words hit you just as they are intended to.

Although he didn't allow me to read all of it, because the surprise element is what he likes to keep till the end, I am sure everyone of them is worth reading.

This book is a result of constant persuasion from his friends to publish his works because he deserves it.

Preface

Love is something hard to define. The human tendency is to find someone who is compatible and ready to align with you, accept you and be with you for the way you are. Finding someone like that is a blessing or, should I say, a dream come true. Stories make us realize how chance encounters change into a lifelong affection, How friends who have known each other for years realize that they are more than just friends & how from enemies/strangers, two people come close enough and never part ways again.

Love stories are not just a figment of the imagination, and they are the proof of varied colors that your heart carries within it.

"LOVE & ALL OF IT" presents you with a bunch of short romantic poems.
Some of them, apprehended from real-life situations, from people I know, and some of them just another colored canvas from my imagination.

I will leave it up to you to decide which one is real and which is fictional because when you read, you connect, and you realize that all of them could be you, but when and where is all that matters.
Let Love find its way to you as you read them and

drop your feedback, comments to me on rahul.bhole@nift.ac.in or my Instagram page inked_heights_.
Moreover, let me know which poem connected you the most.

Enjoy this wild ride of Love & Romance that will take you through a varied range of emotions and make you live every word as you read.

RAHUL V. BHOLE

Acknowledgements

I would like to thank a handful of people who have supported me all along in my dream of becoming a writer.

Firstly, my Mom & my Dad, who has always been supportive of my work and never doubted my ability or questioned my passion for writing.

Friends always play an important role in motivating you towards your goal and I would like to take this moment to thank them for unconditional and rigid support which kept me going all this time.

Prerna Gupta, Shalini, Navya Gupta, Jagdish, Twinkle Lalwani, Himani Chauhan, Mitaali Dayal, Twisha, Ashi, Ishita, Dishant, Shama to name a few and many more.

My sisters, Dhanashree & Medhavi have always supported me with my endeavors.

This book is a result of the constant motivation provided by you guys. It would have been impossible for me to write it all and bring it to a conclusion.

Thanks for your contribution to making this dream into reality.

Introduction

Romance and Love is an ever green topic and something that mostly everyone relates to in different ways. Everyone atleast has had a crush in their life time and the feelings that one experiences are something different.

It's been 7 years since I took up writing and the main reason behind romance being the topic I like to write on is interaction with people and their stories which people narrate to me and my personal experiences ofcourse.

This book brings out some of the best peoms that I feel everyon will connect to in some way or the other.

Love has many faces which people tend to ignore because it not always is just -"_Happily ever after_".There is more to it than we realize and know.
As they say, Love is the simplest yet the most complicated emotion to understand and comprehend.

Experience love in a new way with me and feel it the way you have never ever done.

ONE LAST THING

One last meet, and we might not meet again.
One last breath and I might not breathe again.

One last hope, because I might not need it again.
One last tear, because I might not cry again.

One last smile, because I won't smile again.
One last call, because I won't call again.

One last heartbreak and it will never break again
One last word and I will never speak again.

One last day and I won't live again

- Rahul V. Bhole

MOMENT OF LOVE

Catch up the moment, never to be back,
Grab the train, of emotions get on track.

Let the infectious love from her smile give your secure heart a hack.
Let the hardened feelings crack.

Let yourself fall in love,
push that dumb mind of yours in a sac.

*Oh come on, you love her, just say it out loud,
Fine don't shout, just think it out aloud.*
Because reaching out to a heart,
With words unsaid is an art.

Let the touch from her fingers ring a chill down your spine,

Turn around and stare in her eyes, don't utter anything else
Except a kiss and with your eyes closed and your heart shouting be mine.

- Rahul V. Bhole

BROKEN HEARTS

Those last words hit him hard.
Not scratching, but ripping him apart.

She hardly cared about what she said.
Did it even strike her
if his feelings were left able enough to love
or were they left dead?

No texts, no messages went unnoticed for a day or two.
Something started bothering,
dark thoughts started to linger on,
and then pass through.

Tensed and bothered,
she found her steps to his street.
Fears came alive,
and tears turned up with life.
White clothes and a gathering was what met her eyes in a
distant haze
The crumbled paper clutched in her hands felt like glaze

Steps retreated and everything went blank.
The realizations of her actions made a chill run down her
spine and freeze her
soul.

Did her utterances hurt him more or was it the whack, that
left fingers distinguished on his face, which still had a smile
as he stood by the pole?
Although he didn't reflect but was he left broken so bad,
never again to the whole?

The days that followed were no better,
until the day her eyes caught a sight that made her heart
skip a beat
and body burn with heat.

He stood there, amongst his friends with a smile although
faded and grey.

She wanted to control but she could not and dashed
towards him as her hands hugged him tightly.

Today it did feel right,
the same face she had slapped that day,
today was in direct contact with her lips.

They were indeed a sight but he pushed her aside.
She was not expecting that, and all he said was - "broken
hearts don't usually look back".

- Rahul V. Bhole

AND WE END HERE

Today it has come to an end after a long wait.
It's something I don't want to believe and what I hate.

Things turn out to be weird and unsaid.
Faces and feelings left unread.

It's been a year since we met and my sentiments rendered
an epicentre to start from and finish off on her.

That poetry where words once danced, silence behold,
Those characters developed upon her, appear lifeless as
they stare back with a story left midway, before it could
unfold.

Emotions crushed, broken dreams safely which I had kept
are now scrapped,
waiting to be swept.

Yes, it's been done today, but I'll act as if, it's been a while.
Wounds are fresh, but I'll still manage to smile

- Rahul V. Bhole

TOGETHERNESS

It's been a while,
As I look at her face,
Everything is distant and
Lost in a haze.
But,
Without those specs sitting on my nose,
I can still identify her face.

50 years of togetherness,
And still, the memories never fade.

Her love for me
and her presence in my life
It like a cherry on the cake.

- Rahul V. Bhole

PROMISE

She said,
Not too far away,
Whatever you have in mind
Just close your eyes and say.

For you to be mine
Is all I pray.
Just for a moment?
No,
It's what I ask for
Every single day.

- Rahul V. Bhole

JUST SAY

She said,
I am not too far away,
when I listen to you pray, every day.

Whatever you have in mind
Just close your eyes, and say.

Her touch was different, hard for words to convey,
and,
All I could say was,

For you to be mine, Is all I pray.
Just for a moment?
No,
It's what I ask for
Every single day.

- Rahul V. Bhole

THANK YOU

Those last words hit him hard.
Not scratching, but ripping him apart.

She hardly cared about what she said.
Did it even strike her
if his feelings were left able enough to love
or were they left dead?

No texts, no messages went unnoticed for a day or two.
Something started bothering,
dark thoughts started to linger on,
and then pass through.

Tensed and bothered,
she found her steps to his street.
Fears came alive,
and tears turned up with life.
White clothes and a gathering was what met her eyes in a
distant haze
The crumbled paper clutched in her hands felt like glaze

Steps retreated and everything went blank.
The realizations of her actions made a chill run down her
spine and freeze her
soul.

Did her utterances hurt him more or was it the whack, that left fingers distinguished on his face, which still had a smile as he stood by the pole?
Although he didn't reflect but was he left broken so bad, never again to the whole?

The days that followed were no better,
until the day her eyes caught a sight that made her heart skip a beat
and body burns with heat.

He stood there, amongst his friends with a smile although faded and grey.

She wanted to control but she could not and dashed towards him as her hands hugged him tightly.

Today it did feel right,
the same face she had slapped that day,
today was in direct contact with her lips.

They were indeed a sight but he pushed her aside.
She was not expecting that, and all he said was - "broken hearts don't usually look back".

- Rahul V. Bhole

DREAM

I will hold your hand,
and dance all night.

Till the sun is down,
and we are surrounded by street lights.

Stars in the sky will light up bright,
your hands around my neck
and my hands holding you tight will be a sight,

- Rahul V. Bhole

THE DAY I LOST

She was there,
But she was still,
She was loosing
I had the will.

She was giving up,
Her hand felt light
But I wanted her to fight.

Memories were flashing,
My screams were lashing.

Words left unsaid,
Tears flowing down,
My eyes were red.
I was there,
Beside her bed.

I held her hand for as long as I could go on.
The line was weak, I felt bleak
and then, it went flat
She was gone,
My world turned black

- Rahul V. Bhole

FOREVER THE SAME

Love you forever,
Love you endless,

Leave you? Never
That's what you said,
when we met by the River

A wanting, a sort of urge,
was what you used to trigger.
With that look,
getting me to dive
in your eyes, deeper.

Feelings might change,
Emotions remain the same.

I still am In love,
For you, I guess it was all but a game.
Deny as much you can,
Still You know,
If you return, I ll still love you the same.

- Rahul V. Bhole

WE ARE SENTIMENTAL

We boys are more sentimental than we say.
Our feelings are much more sensitive than we say.

A cute "hii" from our crush leaves us in an excited state.
We like to try harder every day. We don't leave things on fate.

When a relationship is torn apart, We show ourselves as strong,
but deep inside, softness is what sits in our hearts.

We comprehend you try hard,
and we too try our best, But occasionally,
our efforts go unnoticed.
Not because you don't care or acknowledge them.
It's because we just don't know how to and when to express them.

We are more anxious than you know when your fingers touch our hands.
The moment we try, our heart is on for a race.
We hesitate more than you do to hold that hand in a public

place.

Talking about dance? The hesitancy to slip your hands on your waist as you step close with every passing minute of your favorite song increases.

We try, our hands do muster up the courage but then your hands round up our neck, and our body freezes.

We don't recognize it but,
We need you, more than you know.
We need a hug at times, more than you know.
We cry secretly when you shout, more than you know.

We are sentimental and we know, that is why to everything, you say we agree and bow.
You mean a lot many things to us,
we just don't show.

- Rahul V. Bhole

A BIT TOO LONG

Seems like a bit too long, the wait to talk,
from the last reply
to the next blue tick all along.

Giving chills down the spine,
every time I hear it is that specific song.

To know you, with all the chats is the latest quest.
But then I stop, thinking, maybe next time, for the rest.

Thoughts vibe, interests match,
and the suspense thrives,
with each conversation new facts unfold.

Few known, few untold.

- Rahul V. Bhole

DREAMS ALIVE

I keep those dreams alive,
Yes, the one in which we both strive to survive.
Differences left behind as we make a new start.
With a small place in our heart.

Running up and down every day, nothing to complain
about but a lot more to say.

Your hands encompassing the coffee,
my hands holding you as the winds blow.
Creating a beautiful world of our own, from the seeds we
sow.

Looking at you every day,
I fall in love over and over again.

Hairs all set on a side,
ready to be dried
as you come in,
all drenched from the early monsoon rain.

You with me feels like I could not have asked for more.
I love you from the bottom of my core.

- Rahul V. Bhole

BEFORE WE MEET

(Oh yes, it's the first time we are meeting right?)

Let days change to nights,
when the moon shines bright.

Let the world sleep in peace,
while we enjoy a night with our faces being kissed by the
cold breeze.
Let's just stop, take ourselves on a break to ease.

Yes, I want to present you with flowers, not roses, it's a
cliche,
that's what I'll say.....
However, white lilies might just look good in a bouquet.

Yes, I want to surprise you from dusk till dawn.
I want to see that smile widen as the evening moves on.

Yes, I wanna spend some time with you,
my hands in yours, as we feel the grass and the late-night
dew.

Yes, I wanna stare at you, as you talk,
hands close by,
fingers interlocked as we walk.

- Rahul V. Bhole

GIVE IT A CHANCE

Lets get on together,
I promise it will be better.

Even if it was a mess before,
I still want it a bit more.

Come knock on my door,
Pick me up,
helpless on the floor.

Hide my tears in a hug,
If I stray away,
Give me a hard tug.

Give it a chance,
Run your eyes over
 that album we made,
Give it a glance.

I wanna enjoy my life
Just like our first dance.

- Rahul V. Bhole

STAY WITH ME

Stay with me for a bit more long
For I am here to dedicate you a song.

Ups and downs, highs and lows
You have been a support all along.

You know my story,
I am someone who never hides,
Baby,
Even a coin has two sides.

Hugging you, holding your hand,
I have been on numerous rides.

Leave or stay,
I'll accept whatever your heart decides.

Stay with me for a bit more long
For I am here to dedicate you a song.

- Rahul V. Bhole

THE FRAME

Everyday, I hold you in my hands,
Stroke your cheeks and feel your hairs.

You listen to me everyday,
and never interfere.

And then I put you back in the frame,
beside my bed, when I find coming from my eyes,
a flow of tears.

- Rahul V. Bhole

GONE

The glass is what stood between us.

I could see you, but you were far away.
I wanted to talk, but you had moved on.

There were things I wanted to say.
Maybe I could have tried,
But I knew things were long gone.

- Rahul V. Bhole

THE NOTE

He left just one note for her, on the last day, before he left.

"I would like to live one life with you,
rather than a hundred with someone else."

"I would like one hug from you,
rather than a hundred kisses from someone else."

- Rahul V. Bhole

SOMEONE

Trust me when I look at them, although I do hide,
it does hurt inside.

I too want someone by my side, to hold my hand,
Call me with a zest,
and say "*let's meet today, please?*".
and my answer is, just a tiny giggle on her cute request.

I too want someone to hold my hand as we walk the
market streets,
and pull me closer just to rest her head on my shoulder as
we sit in the park enjoying the.

I don't say it, I never complain, but the vacant seat in front
of me screams out in silence,
for someone to walk in, sit down, hold my hand,
and kiss me just like the setting sun kisses my face,
because sitting alone, even my coffee tastes a bit bland.

- Rahul V. Bhole

THE PAGES OF MY BOOK

The pages of my old book,
Hold my memories of yesterday,
Every smile, every tear,
Every moment spent with you
all those years.
Words that hurt me, brought all those tears.

The pages of my old book book hold all those words,
just as you said Hard and Rash,
Crushing through my feelings,
just like Trash.

- Rahul V. Bhole

NIGHTS WILL BE REMEMBERED

These nights will be remembered when we look back in
time.
These nights will be remembered when we look back in
time.
Sitting in this train with our backs reclined.

Chatting about the world, and all whereabouts,
The coach door open and not a single cloud.

There's only the sound of tracks that rings
in our ears, rest silence is the only thing we can hear.

Sharing the same birth with our best friends,
Lying there chatting on opposite ends.

We'll someday close our eyes and remember those days,
How we enjoyed and we cherished with each .other in all
possible ways,
Which today are lost in a sort of haze.

- Rahul V. Bhole

A SMILE FROM HER

A smile from her is all i want,
there is nothing in this world that I have cherished so long.

Wonders I have seen which have left me astound,
but never like her smile which leaves me spell bound.

Whatever makes her cry, whatever makes her frown,
I'll make sure those things never come around,
and wherever she goes only happiness surrounds,
because nothing on her face but a smile I want.

When I am sad, she holds my hand, gives me a smile,
which helps me walk in my life for miles.

Never will I let a tear drop from her eyes,
becasue that will be the gravest of all my crimes.

To keep her happy is all I want,
For a smile from her is all I want,
because there is nothing that I have cherished so long.

MY FIRST LOVE

I used to stand in a corner, looking at her from one side,
trying to get a peek into her Black - blue eyes.

I was a nerd with an expressionless face,
and she was a girl full of grace.

Years had passed since I fell in love with her,
but hid my feelings out of fear.

It was the 14th of feb. as far as I remember,
when I gathered up the courage to express it to her.

Still something unusual stopped me in my path,
so I just penned down whatever feelings i had in my heart.

Reaching the class, I saw her seated on her desk with the table full of cards,
 friends holding gifts and flowers.

Busy in her talks she suddenly turned towards me and gazed in my eyes,
I hid the paper just in time.

I turned around and walked out in short fast strides,
but she overtook me and stood in front of my eyes.

She took the paper and flapped it open even before i could realize.
She read - "5 years of love hidden inside".

She read it all in an inaudible sound,
until crystal like tears dropped from her eyes to the ground.

She stood still with her eyes shining bright,
and then suddenly hugged me tight.

I was transfixed, confused what to say,
when atlast she said - " Silly, I too love you".

- Rahul V. Bhole

A SECOND CHANCE

A boy was buried in the cemetery today,
and everyone had one last tribute to pay.

One of them, a girl, eyed the tombstone, on which were engraved
some last words that he had to say-

"I will depart now, for I have done my part,
but there is a feeling of sorrow deep in my heart.
This was the date, I remember alright
because for me it was love at first sight.
A year had passed since then, and
I just asked her for a date that night.
She slapped me, not once, but twice.
This insult was far too grave for me to fight,
and I decided to end my life."

"I won't forgive her however hard she tries."

And all she could do was cry,
till her tears turned into a thin stream of blood flowing
down her eyes.

Just then with a loud scream, she sat upright,
and saw the morning sun shining bright.

She felt her eyes which still had some tears,
and the only touch of them brought back her fears.

Her thoughts were interrupted by the doorbell sounding,
once and then twice.

Down the stairs, she ran in short fast strides and opening
the door,
stared in surprise.
For there he stood in front of her eyes.

She ran towards him and hugged him tight,
letting out all those tears that she had held inside.

That day on she never looked back,
in fear of remembering that dreadful night,
when her dreams took away the person, who has loved her
more than anything in his life.

 All she wanted was her hands to hold him tight
and never let him out of her sight.

- Rahul V. Bhole

LET IT GO

Words have hurt, scared your heart,
Forgive him not for breaking it apart.

A grim mistake, yes...But,
Even death once gives a way out.
He can't scream, but, you can feel it aloud.

Hands ache and mind goes round,
with messages from his side, popping like a pile
Sometimes emotional,
Sometimes funny,
Sometimes caring

Just with an aim to make her smile.

Mistakes happen,
Go with the flow
Let him in once,
Let it go.

- Rahul V. Bhole

FOREVER DUE

If she changes the shades of her lipstick,
with the one, you bought just to make you feel good,
she is the one for you.

If she makes you smile,
trust me she is the one for you.

If she cooks you food just to cheer you up,
trust me she is the one for you.

If she changes the music on her home theatre
to something you can dance on,
trust me she is the one for you.

If she listens to you,
without you speaking out a word,
trust me she is the one for you.

If she adjusts economically
and helps you out,
without being asked,
trust me she is the one for you.

If she waits for you, to get a meal together,
just to spend some time with you,

trust me, she is the one for you

If she holds your hand
and pops a peck in public without hesitation,
she adores you,
trust me she is the one for you.

Just stay, don't walk astray,
she has supported you
in more than a million way
and the bills of those emotional moments are forever due.

- Rahul V. Bhole

EYES NEVER HIDE

She looked at me,
Staring In my eyes,

Words trying to barge out,
But something prevented me
From saying it loud.

Her eyes pulling me,
With a force
Convincing enough
 to make me stay
It was hard,
Try as much I wanted
to walk away.

Pulling myself away,
As if hiding a bag of lies

She caught up,
Holding my hand
Turning me around
Said,
"Try as much, your LOVE is what
Your eyes never hide"

-Rahul V. Bhole

I WALK DOWN THE ROAD

I walk down the road all alone today,
Where once you accompanied me only my shadow walks.
I walk down the road all alone today,
Only silence surrounds and my shadow talks.

The cold breeze which once used to irritate me,
Today brings a feeling of calmness inside me,
Around the corner, the dog still stares at me with it's
Large round eyes.

I ignore it yet again and divert my thoughts towards the
sky.
No one's there for miles and miles,
It's just me and my dreams full of smiles.
I walk down the road, all alone today.

The sound of dried leaves falling from the trees.
The sound of birds singing in chorus, and my heart
pumping regularly to remind me that I am still alive.

I walk down the road all alone, every day for hours,
In a hope to shed my old self away and take on a new
form,
I walk down the road all alone, again and again, and again.

- **Rahul V. Bhole**

I DON'T KNOW WHY

I don't know why I have lived so long,
Everything appears so dull and worn, because
You are the one I have missed all along.

Sweet were those days with that morning tea,
When we used to sit in our garden beside the sea.

Standing beside our house were those great banyan trees,
Which swayed along all day with that perfumed sea breeze.

Sunday's were the best with your home- cooked food,
And our champ jumping up like a nasty little brute.

Sitting in the ground and watching the squirrels pick up
our nuts,
and people running in and out of their huts.

All those rain drenched days were a sight ,
when you used to sleep with your head on my shoulder the
whole night.

Those late night coffees with you,
which at numerous occasions bought a smile on my then
tense face,
But today drinking this coffee without you is altogether a

different case.

Today I sit for hours, staring at the stars,
and remember how you walked away from me years ago,
nd gave me those scars.

- Rahul V. Bhole

MOVE ON

He was here,
But you refused to hear.
He wanted to come close
But your actions said don't you dare.

He worked on it, and he did it hard,
Trying to fix a wrongly said part.

His words might be wrong,
Your are right on your part
But even he had feelings,
He had a heart.

Today he is gone,
With a heavy heart,
He had to part,
Because you asked him to move on.

- Rahul V. Bhole

SHE LOVES ME

She loves me,
But denies.

She loves me
 but hides.

She smiles on me,
But keeps it aside.
Slow but bumpy is the way,
But my heart rides.

Be with me
Or walk away,
Stay is what
she decides.

Open up?
Or hesitate,
In me she confides.

Yes,
She loves me,
Yet she hides

- Rahul V. Bhole

NINE

Lost in the bunch of letters that you wrote long back when
you were Mine.
It seems like a long time
and
I had a dream when I was doing just fine.

See me today, broken and lost,
You broke that layer of trust just
as thin as the Early morning Frost.

I go to sleep, with thoughts wandering suddenly to find
you by my side,
But the pillow that buries my dreams,
absorbs the flow of tears and lets them hide.

Late-night was a routine when you were mine,
But now, I sleep at nine.

- Rahul V. Bhole

THE CONVERSATION

She wanted a reason,
He had none,

She wanted them to stay,
But he wanted to run.

Her emotions were at stake,
But all he said ~ it was a mistake.

She thought together
by fate, they were bound,

He said,
Just walk away,
and don't ever turn around.

- Rahul V. Bhole

EDGE OF A CLIFF

There I was, staring down the edge of a cliff.
Mind racing, heart going adrift.

Eyes racing, giving the valley a riff.

The showers were loud, and slapped my back,
I stood for a while rigid and stiff.

I heard a voice -

Life is much more, you just need a tiff.
You jump you lose,
You turn you choose

And there she was,
Watching me,
staring down the edge of a cliff.

- Rahul V. Bhole

HOLD

She wanted a reason,
He had none,

She wanted them to stay,
But he wanted to run.

Her emotions were at stake,
But all he said ~ it was a mistake.

She thought together
by fate, they were bound,

He said,
Just walk away,
and don't ever turn around.

- Rahul V. Bhole

ABOUT HER

Stirring the world with those
deep brown oculus,
Restraining her flicks from covering her eyes
she moves them behind her ears,
her smile mesmerises me
 every time I see her do so.

Her earrings dangling on her side
everytime her hand brushes across them
makes her look like a fantasy
 that every one desires.

Incognizant of all those hearts that are trying to match the
pace of hers,
She walks in every day and all I do is sit and gaze at her till
she walks out,
but that pleasant perfume marks her presence until the
next day.

- Rahul V. Bhole

SMILE

Watch as my heart reaches out to you,
Just feel the vibe, it resonates to you.

It's a different feeling,
I am experiencing something new.

Some unsaid words pass by your side,
My heart takes me on ridiculous ride.

I watch you stand, as I tend to hide.

You seem to me, like a distant Mile
But,
The world spins down and my heart beats on as you look
at me and pass a smile

- Rahul V. Bhole

WISH

Gifts sit and rust,
Memories although slowly,
Turn to dust.

I am craving,
for love to fulfill my thirst.
Tears ready to burst.

I see them turn,
As the letters slowly burn.

There still was a wish,
For you to return.

- Rahul V. Bhole

JUST US

Was it me?
Or was it us,
Fighting over a fuss.

Some words unsaid,
Some letters unread

Yes I hope
for you to be back.
Get my life back on track.

hold my head,
on your lap you keep
Help me sleep,
Let my thoughts
sink in deep

Kiss my head,
As I tend to ignore, blush
And Turn red.

- Rahul V. Bhole

WAITING

I sit there on the worn-out bench,
with the rain pouring hard and watching people drench.

Where once you used to sit,
today a crumbled letter resides.
Scores of people cross my path,
but my tears flow In silence,
and the rain helps them hide.

Getting flashbacks from the past,
one after another, just going on,
with no clues till when they will last.

Those inked words flow away as the rain continues,
the blue ink mixed with water flows down with different
hues.

-Rahul V. Bhole

CHAPTERS CLOSED

Some chapters of my life have unfinished ends,
because the will and wish to finish them
never made it to the end.

Having typed those messages midway,
with questions in my mind,
I still can't finish it
and hit the button flashing Send.

Things are stuck midways
with no solution in sight,
a relationship strained
and broken with the fight.

Although I have spent crying numerous endless nights
Today, I hold on to my tears tight.
because crying for you is something not right.

-Rahul V. Bhole

SOMETHING ABOUT HER

She has been a support for more than a year.
Be it an emotional breakdown or a frustrated mind, she
has always been here.

She knows how to calm me down,
and if I run from problems how to turn me around.

She knows when I need a bit of support and when a push,
She has the ability to make me shush
She knows when I want her to stay online and do mindless
stuff

Although miles apart, we are still close.
Our chats daily are the only fun dose.

Saying hello in a million ways,
helps us laugh and pass our days,

-Rahul V. Bhole

HEAR ME OUT

Just hear me out once,what I have to say,
then I myself will walk away.

Apologies have failed, and so have you,
now just hear listen to my part which is due.

I never walked out on you,
you wanted a break.
I just agreed on a decision,
that I didn't even take.
You broke the bond that we had formed all along.

Don't ask why in place your hand, someone else holds mine.
She knows about you, she knows about us and she is fine.

There was a time
when I would have literally fought,
for you to be mine,
but with her I am doing perfectly fine,
and it's difficult to say if I will ever remember you,
looking back in time.

As I said,
Just hear me out once,what I have to say,

then I myself will walk away.

- Rahul V. Bhole.

RESTRAINED LOVE

You are free to walk away, guilt-free,
from the memories that we made.
Maybe for you, they didn't exist.
But for me, they will be hard to wipe out and fade.

You are free to walk away,
I won't ask you why, but
don't expect me not to cry.

You are free to walk away, surely you can leave,
I don't want any explaining to be done or a word to be heard,
For all my efforts to make you stay have deterred.

I am done trying to hold you back, You are free from my bound,
but I request you, if you walk away today, don't ever turn around.

- Rahul V. Bhole

CLOSE ENOUGH

She Pulled my hairs,
sratched my neck.
I shouted,
What the heck.

Door clicked,
My heart said,
All hands on deck.

Ripping through her hairs,
My ice cold hands run down that spine,
We were drunk,
It was hardly nine.

I asked-
"You push me back,
You bring me close."

"Shusshhh", she said.
"I am not a tulip,
But a black rose."

"Dare not stray away again",
I said pulling her close

- Rahul V. Bhole

FINALLY APART

I got up and packed whatever was mine,
for I knew, I had to leave, it was time.

Not that I didn't mind anything she said at all,
but, I knew this relationship was one-day gonna fall.

I took one last glance at the whole place,
which once we had considered our own private space.

I scribbled a note and left it on the tabletop,
finally locking all the memories inside, I clicked the lock.

Moving all those feelings away from my heart,
I watched as we drifted apart.

My heart was beating fast and feelings were ablaze,
as the house turned into a distant haze.

- Rahul V. Bhole.